Rhapsody in Green

BN
MERRY
HALL

McLaren

RHAPSODY IN GREEN

The Garden Wit and Wisdom
of Beverley Nichols

Edited by
Roy C. Dicks

TIMBER PRESS
Portland | London

To the memory of J. C. Raulston, who started me on my Nichols journey, and of Bryan Connon, who freely shared his Nichols memories and memorabilia; and to Bobby J. Ward for everything else.

Drawings by William McLaren
Compilation copyright © 2009 by Timber Press.
Introductions and index copyright © 2009 by Roy C. Dicks.
All extracts copyright © the estate of Beverley Nichols.
Published in 2009 by Timber Press, Inc.

The Haseltine Building
133 S.W. Second Avenue, Suite 450
Portland, Oregon 97204-3527
www.timberpress.com

2 The Quadrant
135 Salusbury Road
London NW6 6RJ
www.timberpress.co.uk

Design by Dick Malt
Set in Monotype Baskerville
Printed in United States of America
Third printing 2009

Library of Congress Cataloging-in-Publication Data
Rhapsody in green: the garden wit and wisdom of Beverley Nichols /
edited by Roy C. Dicks. -- 1st ed.

p. cm.

Includes bibliographical references and index.
ISBN 978-0-88192-948-5
1. Nichols, Beverley, 1898-1983. 2. Gardening--Anecdotes. I. Dicks, Roy C. II. Nichols,
Beverley, 1898-1983. III. Title: Wit and wisdom of Beverley Nichols.
SB455.G3625 2009
635.9--dc22
2008021744

A catalogue record for this book is also available from the British Library.

CONTENTS

RHODODENDRON
SOULIEI

ERYTHRONIUM
REVOLUTUM

MERTENSIA
VIRGINICA

TRILLIUM
GRANDIFLORUM

INTRODUCTION

I first became acquainted with the garden writing of British author Beverley Nichols in 1992 when a friend lent me a copy of *Down the Garden Path*. That 1932 chronicle of a novice gardener's mistakes and discoveries was addictively funny and heartfelt, with wonderful quips like "I would rather be bankrupt by a bulb merchant than a chorus girl" and delightful descriptions such as "a cyclamen that looks like a flight of butterflies, frozen for a single, exquisite moment in the white heart of Time." I was fascinated by these literary musings that could as easily bring a tear as a smile.

I immediately wanted more, but found that Nichols's gardening books, except for *Down the Garden Path*, had long been out of print. In those pre-Internet days, it took some effort (and financial outlay) to collect his twelve gardening titles. I obsessively devoured each book, marking dozens of hilarious and vivid passages and reading them out to friends, delighting in their enthusiastic reactions.

My book-collecting roused my curiosity about Nichols's life. Research revealed that he was a prolific author, playwright, composer, public speaker and media personality for the majority of his eighty-five years. His works were bestsellers on both sides of the Atlantic for half a century, yet after his death in 1983 they had been all but forgotten. After collecting all sixty of his books, I saw that much of his writing centered around issues of the day that are now of limited interest. But Nichols's garden writing had clearly stood the test of time.

I began a one-man crusade to reintroduce Nichols's gardening works to the public. I approached Timber Press in 1994 about reprints, a project that took a while to get past various hurdles. In the meantime, I started giving Nichols lectures and readings to horticultural organizations across the country to drum up interest. Responses such as, "It was remarkable to see an audience held in rapt attention for an hour" and "Nichols's writings inspired me to work on my own garden with renewed determination" confirmed that there was a large audience ready for a Nichols comeback.

In 1998, Timber Press published the first reprint, and a decade later it had ten in publication. The books cover Nichols's first garden and Tudor cottage in the village of Glatton during the early 1930s (*Down the Garden Path* and two sequels), his city garden in London right before the Second World War (*Green Grows the City*), his Georgian manor house and grounds in Ashtead during the 1950s (*Merry Hall* and two sequels), and his cottage and garden in Richmond, on the outskirts of London, during the 1960s (*Garden Open Today* and a sequel).

The appeal of these books comes from a sense that Nichols is speaking to all gardeners, from armchair to professional, as he boldly sets down his gross failures, extreme infatuations, opinionated dislikes, and abiding eccentricities. He seems to be expressing what most gardeners would not say aloud or admit to others about themselves.

Although Nichols's gardening books are somewhat novelistic, with memorable characters and amusing anecdotes, their cores are Nichols's poetic contemplations, witty epigrams and penetrating observations. Nichols's knowledge and perception come shining through the elegant turns of phrase. Unfortunately, Nichols is not held in high esteem by the literary establishment and often is dismissed by gardening professionals as a dilettante. But true gardeners should find Nichols a most kindred spirit in his passionate responses to plants and nature.

The popularity of the reprints led to this present compilation, drawn from all of Nichols's gardening books (for a complete list of works cited, see pages 12 and 13). Having supplied research and indexing for the Timber reprints, as well as introductions for half of them, I felt privileged to be tasked with making these selections as well. I have grouped quotations by category, such as the weather and favorite flowers, with each excerpt accompanied by its source and page number—and an index at the end of the book will help you to locate quotes by key word or plant name. Nichols generally used the common names of plants, some of which were spelled differently then ("wistaria," "paeony"), and he wasn't overly concerned with conventions of nomenclature (sometimes leaving the E in *Erica carnea* uncapitalized, and even omitting single quotes around cultivar names). However, I have left Nichols's words largely intact so his original voice can come through—errors and all.

Much credit is due Timber Press acquisitions editor Neal Maillet (now Timber Press publisher), whose perseverance resulted in that first Nichols reprint and those that came after it. My work on this volume has been greatly facilitated by the support of commissioning editor Anna Mumford and copy editor Erica Gordon-Mallin.

If you have read dutifully this far, it's time to turn the page and enter the special world that Beverley Nichols so uniquely creates. I envy the first-time reader's initial reactions but I also anticipate the joy of the returning enthusiast.

Roy C. Dicks

WORKS CITED

Below are titles of the home and gardening books by Beverley Nichols from which the excerpts in this volume have been drawn, listed in order of their original publication. In parentheses after each title are the first British publishers and dates, followed by the Timber Press reprint publication date where applicable. A title abbreviation with page number is appended to the end of each excerpt in this volume. The page numbers are drawn from the Timber reprints, or from the original British publications where no reprint exists. (Most American editions of these books have different paginations.) For more information on the life of Beverley Nichols and a complete list of his writings, please refer to www. timberpress.com/beverleynichols.

DTGP—*Down the Garden Path* (Jonathan Cape 1932) Timber Press 2005

ATR—*A Thatched Roof* (Jonathan Cape 1933) Timber Press 2005

AVIAV—*A Village in a Valley* (Jonathan Cape 1934) Timber Press 2005

HDYGG—*How Does Your Garden Grow?* (George Allen & Unwin Ltd 1935)

GGTC—*Green Grows the City* (Jonathan Cape 1939) Timber Press 2006

MH—*Merry Hall* (Jonathan Cape 1951) Timber Press 1998

LOTS—*Laughter on the Stairs* (Jonathan Cape 1953) Timber Press 1998

SOTL—*Sunlight on the Lawn* (Jonathan Cape 1956) Timber Press 1999

CABC—*Beverley Nichols' Cats' A. B. C.* (Jonathan Cape 1960) Timber Press 2003

CXYZ—*Beverley Nichols' Cats' X. Y. Z.* (Jonathan Cape 1961) Timber Press 2003

GOTD—*Garden Open Today* (Jonathan Cape 1963) Timber Press 2002

FFF—*Forty Favourite Flowers* (Studio Vista 1964)

TAOFA—*The Art of Flower Arrangement* (Collins 1967)

GOTM—*Garden Open Tomorrow* (Heinemann 1968) Timber Press 2002

DTKS—*Down the Kitchen Sink* (W. H. Allen 1974) Timber Press 2006

Chapter 1

IN THE BEGINNING

Nichols was a true novice in 1928 when he started on his first garden at the Glatton cottage in Cambridgeshire, England, and in some ways he remained one. With each new home and garden, he maintained his childlike enthusiasm, his willingness to make mistakes—and his extravagant horticultural expenditures.

FIRST BLOSSOMING

MEN COME TO gardens by many roads and learn to be gardeners by many chances. (GOTM, 79)

THE GREATEST SERVICE of the amateur in the art of gardening—or indeed in any of the arts—is that he does things wrong, either from courage, obstinacy or sheer stupidity. He breaks rules right and left, planting things in the wrong soil at the wrong time of the year in the wrong aspect. And usually, we must admit, the result is disastrous. But not always. (GOTD, 185)

AUTHORS SO SELDOM confess to their failures. As a result, their gardens do not really come to life; they have an almost dream-like quality in which the lawns are like softly-lit stages and the flowers dance in the borders like a well-drilled chorus. (GOTD, 77)

·

JUST AS THE best school stories are written by boys who have only just left school, so, I feel, the best gardening books should be written by those who still have to search their brains for the honeysuckle's languid Latin name, who still feel the awe at the miracle which follows the setting of a geranium cutting in its appropriate loam. (DTGP, 9)

·

I HOPE THAT from time to time [gardeners] may be tempted to smile, not unkindly, at the recollection of their own early follies. And I hope that there may come to them, once more, a faint tremor of that first ecstasy which shook them when they learnt that a garden is the only mistress who never fails, who never fades. (DTGP, 10)

·

IT WAS NOT till I experimented with seeds plucked straight from a growing plant that I had my first success—the first thrill of creation—the first taste of blood. This, surely, must be akin to the pride of paternity. (DTGP, 48)

·

I HAD NEVER 'taken a cutting' before. . . . Do you not realize that the whole thing is miraculous? It is exactly as though you were to cut off your wife's leg, stick it in the lawn, and be greeted on the following day by an entirely new woman, sprung from the leg, advancing across the lawn to meet you. (DTGP, 147–148)

·

GRADUALLY MY IMPATIENT desire for immediate results, which is the besetting sin of all beginners, died down. I began to take a joy in the work for its own sake. Until you actually own a garden, you cannot know this joy. (DTGP, 35)

A GARDEN OF ONE'S OWN

TO DIG ONE's own spade into one's own earth! Has life anything better to offer than this? (DTGP, 37)

·

THE DIFFERENCE BETWEEN a plant in a pot and a plant in the soil is the difference between a man in an hotel and a man in his own home. (GGTC, 176)

·

IT IS RIDICULOUS to rent things if you are a gardener; it fidgets you. Even a very long lease is upsetting. I once owned a house with a 999 years lease, and it gave me an unbearable sense of being a sort of week-end guest; it hardly seemed worth while planting the hyacinths. (MH, 19)

SURELY, IF YOU are privileged to own a plot of earth, it is your *duty*, both to God and man, to make it beautiful. (MH, 114–115)

IT IS ALWAYS 'next year' when you have a garden. (ATR, 165)

NURSERY TALES

THOUGH IT MAY sound frivolous, you should have a couple of cocktails before making your tour of the nursery garden, because a slight drunkenness clears the eye and frees the spirit.... If you have one or two excellent dry martinis, well iced, your visit will be far more satisfactory, not only to yourself but to the proprietor of the nursery.... You will swerve, instinctively, towards the lovely coloured gracious things and you will order them without stint. The after effects are terrible of course, but it pays. (DTGP, 185–186)

LONG EXPERIENCE HAS taught me that there never *is* anybody in buildings at nurseries; one trudges about for twenty minutes before discovering a youth who tells one that one wants to see Mr Wilkins, which is all too true, one wants to see anybody at all—but how? Mr Wilkins was last seen, apparently, in the conifer section, so off one trudges for at least a mile, only to be told that he has taken refuge in the cold greenhouses. (GOTD, 72)

.

ONE DOESN'T READ gardening advertisements in moments of cooler judgment. One reads them in an ecstasy of unquestioning faith. That is why everybody should buy shares in seed firms. (GGTC, 61)

.

DISTRUST CATALOGUES. I would not say this about flowers, but I say it most emphatically about trees. The average tree catalogue shows you, as an example of a tulip tree, a specimen that was planted by Queen Anne in Kew Gardens in 1708, and has been deluged with liquid manure ever since. If you order a tulip tree on the strength of that illustration, you will be bitterly disappointed by the slumlike stalk which is eventually delivered to you, by a sulky carman, wrapped in sacking. (DTGP, 185)

.

PAY A VISIT to the nurseries. Every conifer has a definite personality of its own and which proclaims itself from its earliest youth, and to buy a tree, even a baby, from a catalogue is as foolish as to adopt a child by parcel post. (GOTD, 121)

PAYING THE PIPER

I SHALL PROBABLY go bankrupt, with my tastes. But I would rather be made bankrupt by a bulb merchant than by a chorus girl. (DTGP, 79)

.

THERE IS OFTEN a somewhat malicious satisfaction in looking into the windows of flower-shops, if one has a garden, and seeing how much one does *not* have to pay for very inferior specimens of one's own flowers. (LOTS, 243)

.

THE ONLY REAL expense lies in the upkeep—(a generalization which applies not only to plants but to people, to friends and to lovers). (MH, 227)

.

THERE IS THE day-dream when I am a millionaire, able to employ innumerable slaves in creating the perfect garden, waving a hand and saying: 'Let there be balustrades and terraces and fountains, and kindly cover the entire slopes of that hill over with daffodils—*at once.*' (There have been several occasions in the past, when I have forgotten that this was a day-dream, and have begun to put the idea into practice, which is the reason why I shall probably end up in an old gentlemen's home.) (CABC, 119–121)

OH, THOSE CHELSEA Shows, and the tortures to which they subject the owners of small gardens! One wanders round in a state of mounting palpitation, ordering dozens of this and hundreds of that, to the great satisfaction of the bronzed young men behind the ropes. Then one goes home, and looks around, and there is nowhere, but nowhere, to put them. When they arrive, one has to give them away, which may be pleasant, but is extremely expensive. (GOTD, 174–175)

.

ANYTHING FOR A little green. It is the spirit which makes men bankrupt themselves over a pent-house, expending more care and anxiety on a few vines and a tiny bed of bulbs than on the physical and mental welfare of their wives. (GGTC, 17)

.

TO ACHIEVE AN elegant informality in the garden always costs the earth. (GOTM, 218)

Chapter 2

EARTHLY DELIGHTS

In describing favorite plants Nichols is at his most poetic, employing just the right images to communicate a plant's beauty, aura, and impact. His unabashedly emotional reactions give us all permission to indulge in similar responses.

VINES

IF I HAD to confine my choice of creepers to a single family—what a hideous thought!—I should probably choose the family of clematis. And if I were limited to a single member of this family, I should probably choose a *tangutica*. I say 'probably' because these hypothetical decisions are so very painful. (FFF, 16)

.

OH, THAT CLEMATIS! It is like a silver fountain that springs from a dark green bowl, and hangs on the summer air with a mist of stars. (DTGP, 252)

THE WILD CLEMATIS —Old Man's Beard—the billowing smoke of Nature's annual conflagration. (LOTS, 121)

'THERE IS ONE thing to remember about clematis.... If they like you, leave them alone.' An axiom which, I feel dimly, might also have some application to one's dealings with one's fellow man. (GOTD, 187)

.

PERIWINKLE SWIFTLY SPREADS a thick carpet under which absolutely no weed can survive, and yet, for some mysterious reason, it does not seem to throttle any bulbs that are planted beneath it. Moreover, it has an exceptional virtue in that it is a carpet that you can cut as easily as you can cut linoleum; if you see it encroaching too closely on some shrub ... all you have to do is to take a spade and cut a square round the shrub.... I earnestly suggest that you become a periwinklist, without delay. (MH, 113)

.

BOUGAINVILLAEA, THAT LOVELY purple creeper that looks as if Nature had designed it specially to hang out for Coronations, royal processions, and occasions of great pomp and ceremony. (GGTC, 95)

.

I HAVE ONLY to look out of my window to see a miracle. It is an old, hollow, shredded trunk. Its bark is like rotten black cardboard.... Yet through this sad and deathly passage there flows a stream of eager life. For this is a jasmine, and high above the father trunk the branches take on a strange green life. Old, old as the jasmine may be, it still spangles the early September days with quivering stars of

Abutilon milleri

Clematis tangutica

Cobaea scandens

Clematis Nellie Moser

silver, darts and foams and sheds its sweet spray over my wall on many bright mornings. (DTGP, 144–145)

Rembrandt Tulips

BULBS

WHY SHOULD ONE want to go out to dinner when one can stay at home with the snowdrops, and enjoy them in solitude? It took a few million years to make a snowdrop. Surely one is justified in spending a few hours in studying the results? (DTGP, 265)

.

SNOWDROPS STAND ROUND in a tiny square, like ballet girls waiting to dance. (ATR, 246)

.

IT WILL BE generally agreed that the only way in which we can appreciate the beauty of snowdrops is by going out into the garden, lying flat on our backs in the mud, and gazing up at them from below. (GOTD, 44)

.

Bendingdowners. You will not find this word in any botanical dictionary, but it seems to me to fill a long-felt want, because of the extremely large number of flowers such as snowdrops, whose beauty cannot be properly appreciated unless one's body is in a position where the head is measurably lower than the sit-upon. (GOTM, 99)

·

WHEN I LOOK at the cyclamen on my desk, with petals of the palest ivory—a cyclamen that looks like a flight of butterflies, frozen for a single, exquisite moment in the white heart of Time—then I try to think back from the petal to the bud, from the bud to the curling stem, from the stem to the first, fan-shaped leaf, and from that leaf to the tiny seed. (DTGP, 213)

·

[THE MINIATURE CYCLAMEN] were engaged in a game of hide-and-seek among the ferns, for the wind had risen, and the ferns swayed backwards and forwards, so that there were moments when they were almost hidden, and one only saw a gleam of pink among the green....I decided that there were few more profitable occupations than watching cyclamen playing hide-and-seek; part of every day must definitely be set aside for it. (SOTL, 86)

·

THE CLUMPS OF autumn crocuses, which had been planted in drifts, in the wood...looked like a sort of celestial laundry, laid out to dry. (AVIAV, 207)

·

[THE] DRAWBACK TO having too many lilies is that they insist on a party being given for them, and since they are so grand and elegant you have to try to be grand and elegant too, and that means dinner jackets, and hiring masses of very ugly silver, and it is all inclined to be rather expensive. (MH, 192)

·

THE REGAL LILIES do indeed praise the Lord. Some of my own, last summer, were so exultant that they praised Him through no less than thirty snow-white trumpets on a single stem, and even the most accomplished angel could not do much better than that. (FFF, 44)

·

I CANNOT IMAGINE what life would be like without the perennial enchantment of the lilies, picked from the garden, carried indoors, set in front of mirrors . . . and gloated upon. Sniffed and savoured, preferably in solitude, examined under magnifying glasses, and, of course, set to music. (DTKS, 175)

·

[*Nerine bowdenii*] is tougher than you would think. After a night of frost, which has blackened the dahlias and made even the hardiest chrysanthemums look a little sorry for themselves, she will greet you in the morning with a rosy smile, her enchanting maquillage untarnished. (FFF, 56)

·

Galtonia candicans . . . on an August night, when the moon is full, there is an almost ectoplasmic radiance around its petals. (FFF, 35)

How CAN ONE ignore ... that singular and faintly sinister blossom *Iris sibirica*? This latter flower can certainly claim to be 'exclusively' dressed; for the petals of no other blossom has Nature designed so curious a fabric, veined with slate and violet and purple. (FFF, 40)

·

ONE OF MY grandfathers died of a clump of *iris stylosa*; it enticed him from a sick bed on an angry evening in January, luring him through the snow-drifts with its blue and silver flames; he died of double pneumonia a few days later. It was probably worth it. (MH, 17)

·

EACH STAGE OF our lives has its 'signature' flower, and those of us who keep diaries would have little difficulty in assigning to each year those flowers which are especially evocative.... Fritillaries are linked with my years as an undergraduate, because in the meadows of Magdalen [at Oxford University] they grow as profusely as anywhere in England.... Year after year, for generation after generation, these flowers have danced in the background through the lives of England's youth. (FFF, 28)

·

IF YOU CAN keep the conservatory ten degrees above freezing point, you can pick arums soon after Christmas, with great benefit to your spiritual life. With even one arum in the room it is impossible to think wicked thoughts; it would be like swearing in front of a nun; and if you do have a wicked thought, in spite of the arum, you must go out and have it in the hall, closing the door gently behind you. (MH, 180)

.

IF YOU REALLY want your heart to dance with the daffodils you must draw squares, triangles and odd shapes in the soil, you must pack those shapes to the brim, you must put in at least six times as many daffodils as you expect to see, and then—ah then, when April comes, your heart will dance, lightly enough! (DTGP, 229)

.

ONE SPRING DAY when I was rummaging about in the orchard, I saw a gleam of yellow under the old chestnut tree. I realized that this must come from some of the daffodils that had been given to a friend to 'hide'. . . . Every autumn, when the new bulbs arrive, a proportion of them are handed out to any friends who may be around so that they may plant them in some secret place, where I can have the fun of discovering them in the spring. It is a sort of floral hide-and-seek which is vastly entertaining. (MH, 112)

.

AS WE ALL know, the only way to plant daffodils is to pile them on to a tray, and then to run out into the orchard and hurl the tray into the air, planting them exactly where they fall. There may be other, less orthodox methods; if so they should be spurned. The tray, the ecstatic gesture— that is the only sure road to success. (MH, 171)

PERENNIALS

IF YOU HAVE a nice clump of foxgloves in your back garden you cannot ever be bored. There is the echo of all the sweet and liquid sounds of the country in their pale bells. In addition, I am told that their roots, if boiled and added to the soup, are guaranteed to make your most disagreeable enemy expire in considerable discomfort within twenty-four hours, but I have not tested this personally. (DTGP, 277)

·

THE SILVER CENTAUREA—that strange plant whose leaves seem ice cold even in the heat of July, and are always stiff and shimmering, flaunting their frosty beauty in the heat of the most ardent suns. (AVIAV, 28)

·

THESE ARE MINIATURE varieties of the common maidenhair [fern] …and some of them are so thickly embroidered on the underside with tiny spores, that through a magnifying glass they look like the most elaborate satin brocade that ever graced the Court of Louis XVI. (GGTC, 173–174)

·

A CLUMP OF paeonies, to its owner, is something that is deeply rooted in his heart. These flowers are part of himself. … The owner of those paeonies has slaved for them, sacrificed himself for them, sometimes, I think, taken years off his life for them. They are not just 'for cutting'.

They are for living with, and maybe for dying with, too. (LOTS, 231)

·

BY FAR THE most brilliant silver in Nature is afforded by [*Senecio cineraria*]. If you dropped a scarf of silver lamé on the lawn, on a cold night, and came out in the morning to find it shimmering with frost, you would reproduce the effect very prettily. When you set it side by side with one of the more common silver-leaved senecios, such as the species *leucostachys*, it shines with an almost arrogant brilliance and the poor *leucostachys* looks as drab as the little girls in the advertisements whose mothers have not used the right washing powder. (GOTD, 138)

·

Senecio Cineraria RAMPARTS. This must be the mainstay of any grey group; even on the dullest days the leaves have a luminous sheen. In full sunshine they sparkle like newly minted metal and by moonlight they glow like the wings of a moth. (GOTM, 96)

·

THE OLD RAMSHACKLE orchard was glistening with cowslips, thronging through the long grass grouping themselves, joining hands, dispersing, reappearing in duets and trios, as though they were obeying the directions of some shadowy choreographer. Cowslips are one of my ninety-nine most favourite flowers. (DTKS, 76)

MY FIRST ASPARAGUS bed was planted with three-year-old roots—to buy roots that were only two years old was unthinkable; before one could pick a bunch one would be dead or stricken with the palsy, or in the middle of war. (GOTD, 90)

.

FOR MORE MODEST decorations, I would recommend another grass, which must surely be among the most delightful conceits ever devised by Nature. . . . This small charmer is afflicted with the name of *Pennisetum villosum*. Why it should be so burdened is a mystery, for when it is in seed it produces feathery nonsenses which suggest the tails of very small and ethereal rabbits bouncing in and out of a Disney playground. (GOTD, 204)

.

[*Dianthus* WHITE LOVELINESS] . . . is a flower which might have been traced on the window-pane by the fingers of the frost. The petals, as you observe, are indented with miraculous delicacy, and the whole blossom is as light and ethereal as any of the young ladies in 'Swan Lake'. However, if we are seeking for comparisons, perhaps the nearest we shall get is to one of those highly magnified photographs of snowflakes. (FFF, 23)

.

PANSIES . . . ARE HIGHLY therapeutic in conditions of nervous stress. . . . Take out a chair on a summer evening, when there is thunder not only in the skies above you but in the whole world of men, lie back and let your eyes wander at will. All those faces! ... You find yourself making up stories about them, you send them marching on great adventures, and even if the thunder growls, it seems to come from over the hills and far away. (FFF, 63)

·

THE LOTUS—A FLOWER born to float like a swan on the surface of the lake, a flower whose petals demand the mirrored flattery of the water and the cool consolation of the leaves. (TAOFA, 18)

·

THE PULSATILLAS ... have the added charm of growing old gracefully; as soon as they have reached maturity they adorn themselves in the most elegant silver wigs, fashioned from the seed pods. When summer is gone, the wigs blow off with the first winds of winter, float far and wide, and eventually transform themselves into families of new pulsatillas. A more graceful method of perpetuating the species, you will agree, than is habitual among human beings. (GOTM, 116)

·

A NATURALIZED WILD flower which should be in everybody's garden—*Mimulus guttatus* ... Why anybody every called it a monkey flower is something of a mystery; if we were in search of an animal metaphor I would have settled for a sort of mad yellow spaniel, with its tongue hanging out. It grows in shadow or in sunlight, in damp soil or in dry and once it has decided that you are a friend, you will never get rid of it. (GOTM, 144–145)

.

ORCHIDS . . . ARE NATURE's shameless assertion of the doctrine of art for art's sake. (GOTD, 193)

.

THE ORCHIDS WHICH you can grow are called *Pleione formosana. . . . My* orchids—I feel I have a sort of proprietary right in them—are not primarily designed for bosom-coverage, though they have looked enchanting on some, in their time. They are meant for gloating, and wonderment, and only on rare occasions for picking. (GOTD, 193)

ROSES

THE HEDGES ARE starred, spattered, enamelled—any word you like—with wild roses—for the roses need many words for their many ways—words that light on the page as delicately as they swing on their branches—words that flush and pale and flush again, as the roses glimmer from white to deepest pink. (ATR, 199)

35

THE LEMON PILLAR catches your attention and you realize the odiousness of comparisons, for this is a rose that is
moonlit even in the blaze of noon. Stand over it, shade it
from the sunlight, and it shines with a secret phosphores-
cence. (MH, 239)

.

CONSIDER THE CLIMBING roses...after three or four years
they were peeping into the upper windows, pressing their
heads against the panes as though they were trying to see
what was going on inside, and I cannot think of a more
graceful compliment that a flower could pay to a man
than to seem to seek entrance into his house. (MH, 240)

.

THE MOST FEMININE flower in the world is *Rosa gallica*,
Duchesse d'Angoulême. There is nothing brave or bold
about this beauty; she is of the palest pink, with petals
of striped silk, she blushes in the sunlight, and she is
inclined to droop her head. When she does this, you may
fear that she is swooning; not at all, it is merely her way.
(GOTD, 102)

SUCCULENTS

THE COLOURS THAT you will find in cacti are colours to
be found nowhere else in the world.... It is as though
Nature kept a special part of her palette reserved from
them, and whenever she happened to mix anything extra

striking or bizarre, said to herself, 'Nobody but a cactus could wear *that*'. (GGTC, 263)

.

THERE ARE ALL sorts of materials in Nature, from the velvet of the pansy to the parchment of the magnolia. But for *silks*, pure, glistening, of the highest quality, you must go to the cactus. (GGTC, 264)

.

THIS FLOWER IS a startling proof of the fact that when Nature decides to be vulgar—really vulgar—she can achieve effects of almost blinding beauty. For nothing could be more opulent, more blatant, more shamelessly exhibitionist than a bed of mesembryanthemum in full bloom. Magenta jostling scarlet, screaming at cinnamon, fighting with shocking pink, yelling against a dozen shades of orange and vermilion. (FFF, 51)

SHRUBS

IT IS NOT too much to say that if you were allowed no other shrub in your garden but the berberis, you could confidently expect to be in a state of mildly hysterical pleasure for nearly three-quarters of the year. (MH, 115)

.

THE WORLD LOOKS quite different if you view it, calmly and objectively, from the shelter of a large rhododendron blossom, with a sort of scarlet tent over your head, and a speckled rug under your feet—though it is rather alarming when bumble-bees, the size of bullocks, peer in at the entrance, and buzz like sirens. (SOTL, 149–150)

．

IT MAY SOUND affected to describe [the 'Lady Chamberlain' rhododendron] as a carillon in coral, but I can think of no other metaphor, for the branches are thickly hung with coral bells which seem, when the wind touches them, to be making music. (GOTD, 69)

．

OF ALL THE chores in the garden, I find [dead-heading rhododendrons] the most agreeable. . . . I let the blossoms tumble to the earth so that they form a glowing pool of colour which makes them look, from a distance, as though Monet had been wandering around with a loaded brush. (GOTD, 70)

．

I WAS GOING through a period of acute fuchsia intoxication—and indeed I still am. Fuchsias are among my ninety-nine most favourite flowers. . . . I could go on for hours, and probably shall, one day, about their white petticoats and their crimson ruffs and the incredible grace with which they dispose themselves. (SOTL, 193)

．

FOR MANY OF us fuchsias are among the earliest flowers to which memory reverts . . . because, of course, we loved to 'pop' them. Even to this day, when Mr Page the gardener is not looking, I find it difficult to resist the temptation of bending down and giving a quick pop to one of the buds. This may not do the flower much good; one can only hope that it doesn't do it much harm. Anyway, this is the sort of thing, perhaps, that helps to keep one young. (FFF, 31)

·

[KALMIA] IS SURELY one of the most beautiful shrubs in Nature, with leaves like a myrtle, and tiny waxen flowers, not unlike a pink lily of the valley, gathered together in closely packed trusses. They would look exquisite under a glass case on a Victorian mantlepiece. (GOTD, 80)

THE SEXUAL PROCLIVITIES of the holly, particularly the lovely variegated gold and silvers, are remarkable, and suggest that they should be made the subject of an inquiry by a sort of horticultural Wolfenden Committee. For example, if you bought a Golden Queen and a Silver Queen you would naturally expect that they would at least have feminine tendencies. But no—both are firmly male. Golden King, on the other hand, is female. Curiouser and curiouser. Who thinks these names up? (GOTD, 84–85)

·

IF THERE WERE a disease called Hydrangeaitis I should have it. Hydrangeas have been giving me pains in the neck and aches in the back—to say nothing of an appalling inferiority complex—for as long as I care to remember. (FFF, 39)

·

A CLUMP OF *Erica carnea aurea* has foliage of such brilliant gold that soon after Christmas it gives the illusion of sunlight on the lawn. (GOTM, 38)

·

ONCE A HEATHER garden is established there is nothing to be done but sit down and enjoy it or—if we are in a sportive mood—to lie down and roll on it. (GOTM, 42–43)

·

WHAT OTHER FLOWER has so sure and masterly a manner with weeds? The *erica carnea* treats these tiresome things with a most elegant disdain; like a rich and lovely woman at a matinee, spreading herself out, so that her cloak and her mink and her accessories gently smother her neighbours. (MH, 155)

IN THE DISTANCE [there was] something that looked like a house on fire. It *was* a house, and it *was* on fire—with camellias. From the gravel path to the bedroom windows they blazed, twenty feet up, painting the walls pink and white and coral. (GGTC, 112)

.

ONE CANNOT HAVE too many camellias, just as one cannot have too much caviar. (GOTM, 242)

TREES

THE FINEST MIMOSA I ever saw . . . was so covered with blossom that it looked like an immense gold powder puff. One could stand under it, and gently shake the branches, so that the delicate dust drifted on to one's head, and one enjoyed all the sensations of a blonde—whatever they may be. (DTGP, 218–219)

.

AN IMMENSE DOUBLE white cherry, at that ecstatic moment in its existence when the sun is telling it that it cannot keep so much beauty to itself any longer, that it is high time it let the sad world gaze upon its innocence. (GGTC, 55–56)

.

THE SKY WAS very blue and the sunlight danced in and out of the branches of the great willow. There was such a multitude of shifting lights, so many swift sarabands of shadow, that you would say some giant and ghostly hand

was poised above it, scattering confetti through the tan-
gled boughs, confetti of gold and silver, that melted into
the summer airs. (GGTC, 66–67)

.

THE INDIAN BOY is the result of a curious convolution
of branches in an old chestnut: there are two perfectly
formed legs, a long slim body, a small knotted head,
and two branching arms uplifted to the sky.... The only
drawback is that in order to [see the boy] you have to be
lying in the bath.... But very few other people have seen
him.... 'If you come up and lie down in the bathroom
I'll show you my little Indian boy—' No. Definitely not.
(MH, 242–243)

.

THE GROUP OF spindles . . . were quite breath-taking
in their beauty, and a perfect example of the way in which
Nature can be vulgar and get away with it—for what
could be more garish than a berry with a magenta shell
and a bright orange pip? (LOTS, 202)

.

THE VERY THOUGHT of the Eucryphia makes my
blood-pressure rise, and fills my brain with a buzz of
superlatives.... The Eucryphia is summer snow. It is
spring blossom in the heavy, sultry months, when the
year is middle-aged. At a time when all the trees in the
valley are staid and set, and when some of their leaves
are already flecked with the sad stains of autumn, the

Eucryphia arrive—young and gay and white—like a girl who has come late to party, and the revels begin all over again. (SOTL, 122–123)

.

AT THE RISK of sounding faintly morbid, as though one had learned one's horticulture from the pages of Baudelaire's *Les Fleurs du Mal*, I must confess that for me the flower of the magnolia is most beautiful when life has almost ebbed from it. These are the twilit hours when the petals flag and falter, when their immaculate ivory texture dims, when they glow with a ghostly radiance that seems to come from another world. (FFF, 47)

.

WHEN I SET out for my daily promenade in Central Park, my path took me past a line of ginkgos ... with the mink-clad armies of Park Avenue matrons tugging their poodles past their indestructible trunks. I longed to pluck the sleeve of one of these matron and say to her, 'Do you realize that you are walking past fifty million years of natural history? Do you realize that if you allowed your poodle to pause at one of those trunks, as he obviously wishes to do, he would be, as it were, sending a personal message, through time and space, to a pterodactyl?' (GOTM, 86–87)

Chapter 3

ENEMIES WITHIN THE GATES

Nichols rarely met a plant he didn't like, but when he did his wit was at its wickedest as he skewered the offender with haughty disdain. On the other hand, his writings reveal a soft spot for even the most widely despised weed.

BEGONIAS ARE NOT flowers, they are a state of mind, and a regrettable state into the bargain. (MH, 53)

.

DATURA ... is a flower that leaves me less than cold. Even in its native habitat in the Mediterranean, where it can grow to its full height and send out a riot of white blossom, it always reminds me of a clump of laurels on which somebody has hung the weekly washing. (MH, 83–84)

.

THE ELM HAD been [the former owner's] favourite tree, and it was he who had planted them, nearly forty years ago. For this alone, he should have been cursed, and so should anybody else who ever plants an elm. They are useless, hulking brutes of trees, and as soon as Constable had finished painting them they should have been rooted out of the British Isles. (MH, 88–89)

·

THE DEVIL'S WALKING STICK. If you wonder why it is called that, the best thing to do is to grasp it firmly round the stem. After which you will probably call it something worse. (HDYGG, 27)

·

IF I WERE artistic dictator of this country I would make it illegal for any householder, during the next twenty years, to plant another specimen of *Prunus* 'Kansan', popularly known as Hisakura, the gaudy double pink cherry which every spring erupts like an infectious rash down thousands of suburban avenues. This shade of pink should never be planted in isolation, particularly against a background of new red brick. Like some of the pinks in the pictures of Matisse it comes into its own only when it is set against less luscious tints—colours, as it were, with a squeeze of lemon in them, to take away the taste of the sugar. (GOTD, 118)

·

IN A SMALL garden, weeping trees—by a curious paradox—are the life and soul of the party. But why must it be a willow, which weeps to such excess? Why not one of the trees whose lachrymosity is less abandoned? (GOTD, 119)

·

NOW FOR ORNAMENTAL grasses. These, I hope you will agree, can be sheer hell. A well-grown 'pampas grass',

sited in the middle of a suburban lawn, with all those
ghastly feather dusters sticking out of it, can be as embarrassing as a middle-aged lady standing on the steps of
a provincial town hall, disguised as Cleopatra after the
annual fancy dress ball at the Rotary Club. (GOTD, 203)

To WHISPER A word against roses, in England or America, is simply not 'done'. When one suggests that we can
have too many of them and that the role they are able to
play in the garden is limited, one's remarks are received
with the same sort of horrified incredulity as if one had
observed, *en passant*, that all dogs were not necessar-
ily the noblest creatures in the animal kingdom nor all
babies the most beautiful examples of God's handiwork.
(GOTM, 152–153)

WHY SHOULD NATURE approve of a hybrid tea? Without
its flowers, which means for the greater part of its life, it

is gaunt, gawky, and deliberately deformed by man, with its tortured, amputated limbs sticking out in all directions, demanding pity rather than praise. (GOTM, 154)

.

A LAWN, WE MUST always remember, is not a natural creation; it is a luxurious artifice, which must be expensively fed and elaborately cosseted. A perfect lawn is a pampered lawn; and pampered lawns, like pampered people, are apt to develop a number of tiresome diseases. (GOTM, 216–217)

.

IF I WERE dictator of this country the only permissible explosives would be reserved for the elimination—with very few exceptions—of our public parks. These explosives would be so powerful that they would destroy every trace of the hundreds of thousands of triangular beds of blue lobelias by which we are at present assaulted, bring instant death to a million shocking-pink begonias, and send into merciful coma, for an indefinite period, the armies of municipal officials who are entrusted by the State with the creation of these monstrosities. (GOTM, 192)

.

DOCKS ARE THE worst weeds of all, because just as you are pulling them up, they make a sickly, sucking noise, and break in half.... Whereupon you have to tramp off to the tool shed, arm yourself with a trowel, and return to the scene of action, only to find that you have forgotten

where the abominable dock-root is lurking. . . . If you are lucky you will find, after ten minutes' search, an obscene sprout that you imagine to be the dock root. It is only after you have thrown it into the hedge that you realize, with horror, that you have destroyed your best gentian. (DTGP, 124–125)

.

GARDENING GLOVES MAY be all very well in their way, but in so many tasks, like weeding, one has literally to take the gloves off. Only one's own nails and fingers can deal, for example, with the sinister little bulbous roots of *Oxalis floribunda*, and only naked arms plunged in up to the elbows can tackle the slimy, sucking growths that have attached themselves to the sides of the lily pond by the time that autumn comes. (GOTD, 14)

.

WHATEVER ITS MEANS of transport the valerian takes root in the crevices [of a wall], sends out its shrill green leaves, and eventually bursts into song in a series of rosy arias round about the first week in July. And the garden will delight in this floral music, and so will its feline neighbours, for whom its aroma has always had a special appeal. And it will go on delighting until one day, with a loud crash, the wall falls down. (GOTM, 139)

.

UNLESS YOU ARE ruthless with [*Corydalis lutea*], your wall will start to crumble and eventually have to be rebuilt. The strength of these weeds, their swiftness and their cunning, is so formidable that . . . I could not help thinking how useful they would have been in a floral assault on Jericho. Instead of that rather vulgar business with the trumpets the affair could have been concluded far more gracefully with a handful of seeds. (GOTM, 140–141)

·

IF WEEDS ARE indeed flowers, and often very beautiful flowers, are we justified in excluding them from the garden scene? Does not the very fact that we do so argue a regrettable lack of imagination? . . . It forces us to examine our whole sense of aesthetic values; it obliges us to ask whether we still have that 'innocence of eye' which is the essential of all artistic perception. (GOTM, 138)

·

THE PRETTIEST DEFINITION of a weed that I ever read was coined by a learned director of Kew Gardens, Sir Edward Salisbury, who wrote, 'A weed is a flower in the wrong place.' Or, more generally, 'A plant growing where we do not want it.' (GOTM, 135)

Chapter 4

BROADENING THE FIELD

Throughout Nichols's gardening writing, he maintains an abiding interest in four specialties: the Lilliputian world of rock gardens, the ecological renewal in planting trees, the extended growing possibilities through greenhouses, and especially the underappreciated joys of winter-blooming plants.

MINIATURE MOUNTAINS

IT SEEMS ALMOST incredible that I could have been such a fatuous and ignorant optimist as to imagine that this was the way to make a rock garden—without any plan, without even an adequate preparation of the soil.... It reminded me of those puddings made of sponge-cake and custard, which are studded with almonds until they look like some dreadful beast thrown up from the depths of the sea. (DTGP, 111–112)

.

WHEN YOU ARE making a Rock Garden ... you must be bloody, bold and resolute. By this I mean that you must stand at a little distance from your slope, visualize a certain broad design, and decide there and then to carry out that design, cost what it may. (DTGP, 114)

.

YOU MUST BE monstrously extravagant with your rocks. By which I mean that you must push them really deep into the earth.... It would be much more soothing to stick the rock on the top of the slope so that you could say 'Look at my enormous rock! How rich I am to be able to afford such enormous rocks!' But if you do stick the rock up like that, you will eventually take a hatred to it. Also, nothing will grow on it, and anyway it will certainly fall down. (DTGP, 115)

.

I HAVE ALWAYS been a fervent advocate of birth-control, but since I have been the owner of a rock garden my fervour has increased a hundred-fold. The prolificacy of the common saxifrage is positively embarrassing. The speed with which the rock rose reproduces itself brings a blush to the cheek. Violas appear to have absolutely no self-control, and as for the alyssum—well, if *we* behaved like the alyssum, Australia would be over-populated before the year is out. (DTGP, 116)

.

THE CHARM OF a rock garden is essentially Lilliputian. To extract the keenest pleasure from it you must be able to diminish yourself—you must acquire the talent for shrivelling yourself up into a creature that is able to walk, in spirit, under the tiny saxifrages, and shiver with alarm at their heavy weight of blossom, to climb, in your mind's eye, the mossy stones, and grow dizzy on their steep escarpments. (DTGP, 123)

.

Now THAT I was once again a regular subscriber to the garden magazines, the advertisements of the rock-garden merchants seemed like a personal affront. Campanulas three inches high—that was one of the things that made me gnash my teeth.... The advertiser *said* they would never be more than three inches high, and for some weeks, at least, one would have the pleasure of believing him. Belief is much more fruitful (and much saner) than doubt. Which is one of the secrets of a happy life. (GGTC, 219)

INTO THE WOODS

To ME ALL woods are enchanted. I cannot imagine being lonely in them.... There are those who shiver and throw uneasy glances behind them when they plunge from the open country into the narrow, tortuous corridors of the trees—and many will skirt the borders of a wood rather than enter its dark recesses. But I feel that the trees are my friends, that I could wander naked among them without hurt, and sleep unharmed among their sturdy roots. (DTGP, 151–152)

THE WHOLE SENSE and spirit of a wood is at once aloof and protective—it retreats from you and yet it shelters too—brushing your cheeks with a sweet caress in spring, laying in autumn a pale, petalled carpet of fallen leaves at your feet, lacing the winter skies with an iron grille of frozen arms. (DTGP, 152)

A BEECH WOOD, which—like all beech woods—was pretending to be a cathedral. (SOTL, 154)

THERE IS SOMETHING lamb-like and poignantly innocent about the shrill green of a baby walnut tree. And all the very young conifers are fascinating, for you can almost see them grow. Half the fun of a wood is this memory of growth—this happy mental catalogue of branches that began as babies, are now reaching manhood, and one day, will shelter you as you creep slowly beneath them towards the dying sun. (DTGP, 184)

.

IF YOU ARE in a position to plant a wood, and if you refrain from doing so, you must be, *ipso facto*, of a bleak and sullen disposition. You are to be shunned. It is arguable that your very existence should be made an offence in law. (MH, 176)

.

PLANTING A TREE is one of the most satisfying things a man can do. When you plant a tree you are perpetuating life, enriching the lovely land you live in, storing up a treasure house of beauty for your old age. (GOTD, 230)

PEOPLE IN GLASS HOUSES . . .

To GO TO the greenhouse when the weather is wild, to close the door, to stand and listen to the wind outside, to the rain that slashes the frail roof, to see, through the misted glass, the black, storm-tossed branches of distant elms, to take a deep breath, to savour to the full the strange and almost uncanny peace which this frail tenement creates—to me this is one of the truest joys which life has given. (DTGP, 210–211)

.

THERE IS NO more agreeable way of spending a lazy hour than by going down to the greenhouse and gravely swivelling all the pots whose plants are craning eagerly to the light. It makes one feel very grand and powerful. (GGTC, 151)

IT IS ALL so exhilarating that one wonders, not for the first time, why people do not live in greenhouses for ever. If everybody lived permanently in greenhouses, nobody—surely—would be foolish enough to start a war. (MH, 145)

.

A FLOWER OR a weed! I do not care whether they *are* weeds, in winter, in the greenhouse, in those little sheltered boxes. It is enough that they are green, that their leaves are like fans, that their stems are of infinite delicacy, with a mist of faint and poignantly adolescent hair, which is gilded by the lamplight. (DTGP, 223–224)

MID-WINTER MADNESS

EVEN IN THE grimmest winter days a garden can give an appearance of discipline, and a certain amount of life and colour, no matter how wild the winds nor dark the skies. (DTGP, 25)

.

THIS PASSION FOR winter flowers has its roots deep, deep within me. I have a horror of endings, of farewells, of every sort of death. The inevitable curve of Nature, which rises so gallantly and falls so ignominiously, is to me a loathsome shape. I want the curve to rise perpetually. . . . I want my garden to *go on*. I cannot bear to think of it as a place that may be tenanted only in the easy months. I will not have it draped with Nature's dust sheets. (DTGP, 52–53)

A buttercup field in mid-January! That is what the aconites will do for you, if you buy enough of them. . . . You cannot have too many aconites. . . . A thousand will make a brave splash of colour, which lasts a month. If you can afford ten thousand, you are mad not to buy them. (DTGP, 63)

·

THE FEATHERY, SPIDERY, yellow exuberance of this darling plant! For was there ever such bravery, such delicious effrontery, as is displayed, on many quiet walls throughout England, by the witch-hazel in mid-winter? Oh, it is much to be praised, infinitely to be exalted, this strong and delicate flower! There is something theatrical about it. To discover it, on a dark day, glistening epigrammatically in a forsaken world, magnificently pert and yellow, is so inspiring that one's hands automatically begin to clap. (DTGP, 66)

·

IF YOU WANT a finer flower than [*Iris unguicularis*] in winter, you had better go and lock yourself up in your greenhouse and sing hymns. (DTGP, 70)

·

I HAD TO be content with protecting a few of the rarer winter flowers. . . . Every night, when I went to bed, I opened my window, and gently lifted in a spray of wistaria, which had clambered up to the glass and was beating its frozen fingers on the pane. (ATR, 168–169)

·

JANUARY WAS GAY and absurdly spring-like. Birds sang. There were sheets of golden aconites under the elm. The snowdrops laughed all day long. Somebody had told them that life was hard and difficult, whereas they found it bland and easy and delightful. (ATR, 175)

THE WINTER JASMINE was still spangled with flowers. They shone there, in the twilight, like late lamps burning in a secret wood. (AVIAV, 273)

THE DARKEST HOUR of the blackest week of the year could not hold me back, could not keep me indoors. . . . Somewhere, on some branch, there would be a bud to be welcomed. Somewhere, in the kindly shelter of a sturdy shrub, there would be the lifted tip of an emerald spear, thrust aloft through the dark earth by an impatient herald of spring. (AVIAV, 285)

OF ALL THE winter flowers I know none is braver nor more trustworthy than the winter aconite. You simply cannot keep it down. I believe that if you asked it, it would come up on an iceberg. In fact, in my garden, it almost did, because once I planted some aconites under a tree and very shortly afterwards the ground was flooded. Then a frost came along, and the ice remained under the tree for weeks. And in spite of this, the aconites came up and actually had the impudence to flower under the ice. (HDYGG, 36)

.

THE WINTER HELIOTROPE is a sort of colt's foot, and very superior persons pretend to despise it. They say that it is dingy in colour—an observation which goes to prove that they are dingy in colour themselves. These critics also complain that it has a bad habit of spreading, and that once you get it in a garden, nothing on earth will ever get it out again. I cannot imagine any sane man wishing to get it out. (HDYGG, 39)

.

THE WINTER HEATHER, *erica carnea* . . . brings the warm glow of August into the depths of winter, and spreads its rosy carpet of blossom with sublime indifference to the frost and the snow. (MH, 153–154)

.

I REFUSED TO admit that there was ever a time of the year when the garden need cease to bloom, that there was not a single day, even in the snow, when it must be shrouded in dust sheets. . . . The best gardeners are three-hundred-

and-sixty-five-day-a-year gardeners, for long experience
has taught them that some of the darkest days can also be
among the brightest. (GOTD, 211–212)

Chapter 5

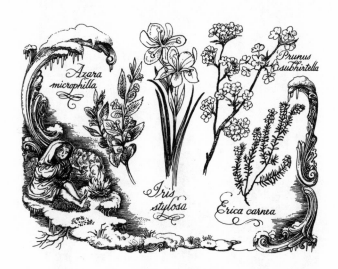

A CULTIVATED CLIMATE

Having grown up in mostly urban areas, the adult Nichols was particularly enthralled by the countryside when he lived or visited there. His enthusiastic interest in weather events and seasonal changes inspired him to pen the most heartfelt paeans.

RESPECTING MOTHER NATURE

THE ONLY 'NATURAL' gardens are those which are covered with weeds and choked with brambles. Learn from Nature, by all means, commune with Nature, take Nature for long and earnest walks down the garden path, but do for heaven's sake keep the blessed creature under control. (GOTD, 38)

.

I MUST CONFESS that the flower show which I love best of all is one which has no roof to keep out the sun and no walls to keep out the wind—the eternal flower show which is staged by Nature, day by day.... For in this flower show there are no labels except the leaves, and often one has to peer very closely, and to study each vein and tendril, in order to read the name that is written on it in letters of green and patterns of pollen. (HDYGG, 19–20)

.

THERE IS NO aroma of D.D.T. in the pages of Jane Austen but her gardens are no less fragrant for the lack of it. The flower-pieces which delight us in the masterpieces of the great Dutch painters of the seventeenth century are often buzzing with insects—caterpillars, beetles, moths, ladybirds and dragonflies—and sometimes I fancy that the artists inserted them not only for their beauty but in order to remind us that they are a vital element in the immensely intricate pattern woven by the supreme artist, Nature herself. (GOTM, 259)

.

AS FOR THE mechanical methods which Nature has contrived in order to spread her progeny, these are so numerous and so complicated that if they had been invented by human beings they would have involved the issue of thousands of special patents. (GOTM, 136–137)

.

WHEN ALL IS said and done the greatest designer of any garden, once the main outline has been established, is Nature herself. That is the heaven of it and sometimes, I think, the hell. The gardener can provide the frame, set up his easel, and sketch the pattern, but as time marches on he must constantly step aside and hand over his brush to Nature. (GOTM, 194)

ALL OVER THE garden, all through the year, Nature is slashing her brush all over the canvas, striking out new lines, hurrying and thrusting and pushing aside, dancing out of the frame, mocking, deriding, but always inspiring. (GOTM, 195)

.

THE DESIGN [a gardener] imposes must be constantly modified and sometimes totally transformed by a hand stronger than his own—the hand of Nature. Maybe the art of gardening is simply the knowledge of how to hold that hand, and how to clasp it in friendship. (GOTD, 25)

COUNTRY JOYS

I WAS FEELING very happy that afternoon. The country was a paradise. The fields were dancing with buttercups, the hedges aflame with the sweet white fires of may. Over the wall the lilac leant its tipsy plumes, giving itself in lazy wantonness to the breeze. Every thrush was a nightingale, that day, and every starling a lark. (ATR, 64)

.

I THOUGHT OF that quiet field, which was so spangled with cowslips in spring that it looked like a sequin cloth, and so buttoned with mushrooms in September that it looked like a coster's jacket. (AVIAV, 75–76)

THIS ETERNAL MUSIC of the English country! It is too quiet to be echoed by any human hands, too subtle to be set between staves or disciplined to the rhythms of art, too delicately coloured to be mirrored in any orchestral score. Eternally it sighs, through field and lane, and every hour a new masterpiece is born. (AVIAV, 103)

·

MOST COUNTRY NOISES I welcome—the shrill arguments of blackbirds in the shrubbery, the patter of big raindrops on the copper beech on a summer afternoon when thunder is abroad, the creaking branches of the chestnuts in the wind, and indeed all the tunes that the wind may play. (MH, 236)

·

THE CURTAIN GOES up at 4 a.m. to a Hallelujah chorus of the birds. When the birds sing Hallelujah it is only common decency to sing Hallelujah too. You cannot do that lying on your back in bed, staring at the ceiling. You have to do it outside, on the lawn, with your bare feet in the dew. (LOTS, 150)

FACING THE ELEMENTS

THE GARDENER'S GREATEST enemy is wind. Not frost, nor snow, nor drought, nor even the sullen implacability of the soil, but wind—the wind that claws and rips at root and branch. (GOTM, 52)

WHATEVER THE WEATHER, however sportive the elements, you can always console yourself by the thought that it is indeed an ill-wind that blows no plant any good.... When the winter is hard, and loath to depart, you can draw your overcoat tighter about you and gain comfort from the thought that no early fruit blossoms are being tempted to make a premature début. (DTGP, 182–183)

·

THERE ARE TIMES when one's desire for blue is so intense that it must resemble the craving of the drunkard for a glass of whisky. Times when one longs to stretch up and up into the heavens, to wrench away the grey casing of cloud that so often imprisons us, to let loose the floods of colour which are glowing behind. (LOTS, 138)

·

THE HEAVENS BLACKENED, and for several hours a violent thunderstorm raged over Meadowstream—a real old-fashioned pantomime thunderstorm, with titans standing in the wings, dropping bricks on to sheets of steel, and the sky's dark backcloth lit with the flickering, electric tails of demons. (SOTL, 205)

·

THE THUNDER GROWLED ever farther away—till its growl was almost a blessing, like the purr of a gigantic velvety cat, prowling the fields and forests. (AVIAV, 176)

THE SYMPHONY IS always the same, and always different. For our conductor is the Weather, and he has as many moods as there are hours. Sometimes he stresses the wood wind, till you would say that there was no sound about you but the high clamour of the elms—sometimes he can bear nothing but strings, and when you go to bed at night you can remember only the way the wind hissed through the rushes on the bank of the stream. (AVIAV, 90–91)

IF YOUR BAROMETER is in the least like mine, it may be likened to a guest who arrives extremely late at a party with news which we have all been discussing for the last three hours. My barometer registers 'Very Dry,' with unfailing fidelity, until the thunderstorm is over. . . . Barometers and politicians, one might say, at random, have much in common. They are always wise after the event. (ATR, 120)

TURNING THE CALENDAR

Spring

ONE OF APRIL's most brilliant days—a day as sparkling as a newly-washed lemon—a day when even the shadows were a melange of blue and orange and jade, like the shadows that poured from the tipsy brush of Monet. (ATR, 34)

.

DRAMATIC IS THE only word for the way spring came, that year. For weeks the earth had been icebound, like an empty theatre. Then, suddenly, the lights were turned on, up above. The delicate fingers of the wind switched away the dust sheets of the snow. And the empty arena filled, as though with cloaks and dresses and scarves, in a thousand shades of green. (AVIAV, 163)

.

THEN CAME THE spring, and the almost unbearable excitement—which can only be enjoyed in an ancient garden—of discovering where the previous owners had planted their bulbs. Of all the treasure hunts in which men have ever engaged, this must surely be the most enthralling. (MH, 170)

Summer

IT WAS A very riotous summer . . . when the sunlight slashed through the trees with the clash of swords, and the heat was arrogant, enveloping. A summer that took its toll

of the flowers, breathing a scornful breath over the droop-
ing roses, so that they gave up the struggle against this fierce
lover, and hung their heads in weary ecstasy. (ATR, 75)

·

THE SOUND OF bees in their hive ... is the Song of Summer. If you listen long enough you will hear all the secrets
the wind whispered as it wantoned through the hedge-
rows. You will understand why the leaves were fluttering,
so madly, against your window at dawn, and why there
was such a poignant sweetness in the scent of the bean
fields. You will hear all the things the flowers never dared
to say. You will hear all the things you never dared to say,
yourself. (ATR, 213)

Autumn

A SHARP FROST overnight, and in the morning a thousand little bonfires will be flickering in all the trees. There
will be tongues of scarlet flame in the maples, and of
yellow flame in the elms; there will be dark fires, deep
in the guelder roses, so that when the wind blows you
see a sombre glow of leafy embers. The sumachs will be
smouldering, the thorns will be ablaze, and in the hedge
at the end of the coppice there will be many fiery miracles
among the brambles. (LOTS, 120–121)

·

THE LIQUIDAMBERS WERE so thickly hung with frosted
cobwebs that their twigs seemed to be *diamanté*, and I

remember thinking that they were really rather over-dressed—all those jewels at so early an hour. (CXYZ, 9)

·

SOME OF THE Japanese maples are inclined to be slightly intemperate in their habits. They are like young men who take one drink, grow red in the face, and become obstreperous. Some Japanese maples do that after their first nip of frost. (HDYGG, 25)

THE MAPLES AND the mountain ashes and the spindles and all the lovely autumn things swell and burgeon and expand, making the most alluring promises of what they will be doing when the frosts come, and dropping, from time to time, a little hint in the shape of a single scarlet leaf that has dressed up too soon, having made a mistake in the date of the party. (MH, 177–178)

·

NEVER WERE THERE such reds, for the maples, as I looked out my window, were *en fête*. They had been giving one of their last parties of the year—you know the parties maples give. All night long, in the keen frost, their faces had been flushed. Then the rain had come, and they glistened in the yellow sunlight. (ATR, 88–89)

Winter

I LOVE A good bonfire, on a December afternoon, when the heart of the fire is like a red jewel, and in the growing darkness the white smoke plumes upwards like the feathers of some fabulous bird. Bonfires, then, are among the rarest joys of man's existence. (SOTL, 196)

·

THERE IS THE tang of ice—the ice that laid out its little mirrors of glass all through the orchard in the clear days of January, so that the sky might lean close and see its face. (MH, 315)

·

SPRING ALWAYS SEEMS to me like a courtship, summer like a marriage, autumn like a really grand party, and winter like a death, and yet a death that has in it an infinity of life. (HDYGG, 22)

NIGHT LIGHTS

FLOWERS, IF THEY are white, will be perfected, transfigured by the light of the moon. The snowdrops will be luminous—a twist of your imagination and you can persuade yourself that they are white elves, met on secret business. (AVIAV, 30)

·

THE SOFT STARS [were] beginning to dust the sky, as though some careless goddess had been making her toilet and had scattered the floor of the night from a silver powder box. (SOTL, 14)

SOMETIMES, ON FROSTY winter afternoons, we take out the braziers and pack them with kindling and coke and a top layer of fir-cones, and light them, and leave them to make a magic circle of warmth. Then, after dinner, we go out, wrapped up, with glasses of mulled claret in our hands, and we sit there enjoying the strangest physical sensations—tingling cold outside, glowing warmth within and all the great heavy curtains of the night about us, with silver sequins in their folds. (SOTL, 177)

Chapter 6

SECRETS OF SUCCESS

Nichols learned and retained a great deal of gardening wisdom over the years, but his gardening books are more than straightforward how-to's. Although he sprinkles his narrative with practical tidbits, he can't resist dressing the advice in wit and whimsy.

LIGHT IN A garden is a quarter of the battle. Another quarter is the soil of the garden. A third quarter is the skill and care of the gardener. The fourth quarter is luck. Indeed, one might say that these were the four L's of gardening, in the following order of importance: Loam, Light, Love and Luck. (LOTS, 76–77)

.

TO LEAVE DEAD pansies on a plant is as cruel as leaving a cow without anybody to milk it. (DTGP, 277)

.

IT IS A very good thing to keep a gardening note-book.... If it were not for my gardening note-book I should never have planted those daffodils in the further meadow, in a bold, brave line, like a golden sword slashing through the fields of spring. I should never have beribboned the banks of the brook with bluebells. . . . I should have forgotten the scarlet oaks, which blaze so fiercely in October that a man may warm his hands at them. (AVIAV, 105–106)

．

Do YOU *wash* your camellia in your city garden? . . . If not, you are a depraved and heartless person. . . . It seems to me strange that you should wash your babies, and not your shrubs. Your shrubs, surely, are more in need of it? *They* have to stay out all day and all night. . . . Washing a tree or a shrub makes it more beautiful, brings out all sorts of hidden colours and unexpected tints. You cannot say that about washing a baby. It just goes on being a monotonous pink. (GGTC, 114)

．

A MAN (DOESN'T) put on gloves when he makes love to a woman. No more he should when he tends a rose. (SOTL, 25)

．

IF IT IS true that it takes God to make a tree, it is equally true that it takes two humans to plant it—unless it is very small and unless you are a very old hand at the game. You want somebody to hold it straight, and most important of all, to jiggle it. (GOTD, 229)

．

YOU SHOULD BE warned that the fruit of [the weeping pear] is quite disgusting; a single nibble of it sets the teeth

on edge for hours. It therefore serves an invaluable pur-
pose as a present for obstreperous infants on those days
when the garden is open to the public. (FFF, 76)

·

I DO BELIEVE very firmly that there exists a 'radiation'—
for lack of a more explicit word—between the soil and
ourselves, and that if this radiation is disturbed we are in
some sense incomplete. There are chalk people, and there
are sand people, and there are people who have an obvious affinity with heavy, sticky clay. And there are people
like myself who demand peat, not merely because they
want to grow rhododendrons but because the moment
they set foot on it they respond to it physically and emo-
tionally. (SOTL, 142–143)

·

EVEN IN A small garden such as mine the quality of the
soil has many variations.... This is especially noticeable
in old gardens, where the ghostly remains of ancient
cemented paths still haunt the beds which the new owners
have dug for themselves, or where the limy foundations of
long-forgotten out-buildings still linger on, to poison the
roots of an unsuspecting rhododendron. Against such a
combination of history and chemistry and sheer bad luck,
the long-suffering horticulturist is impotent. (GOTM, 250)

·

'KNOW THY SOIL' is as vital an injunction to the gardener
as 'Know thyself' to the philosopher. (GOTM, 255)

EARTH

Chapter 7

THE FINE ART OF GARDENING

Nichols's writing is filtered through an artistic perception, his commentaries couched in terms of painting, music, and architecture. He has a highly developed response to the senses and is especially adept at evoking sounds and fragrances.

GARDENS BY DESIGN

LIFE IS MEANINGLESS without some aim, and so is a garden path. By which I do not mean that you have to have some awful little statue glowering at you from the end, or some unnecessary sundial, or a door leading nowhere. All I mean is that if you are walking down the garden path you must walk to *something*, even if it is only a tree, or a gap in the hedge through which you can look out on to quiet fields. (GGTC, 86)

.

EVERY GARDEN PATH can be magically extended if it is made to take a sudden turn to the right or to the left. Which means that somewhere in its course it must encounter a wall, a cluster of trees, even a wooden fence, set there to provoke the eye, to intrigue it, to make one ask the ultimate question—what lies beyond? (GOTD, 27)

·

IT TAKES A very old wall, wrinkled by a thousand rains and winds, enriched by a thousand chance particles of matter, of dust and flying leaf, to offer a shelter in which a flower can really feel at home. Even then, how infinite must have been the number of seeds that have drifted into it, on a summer breeze, before a single one found a resting place. (GGTC, 193)

·

THE BEAUTY OF a square garden begins with the creation of curves, and the beauty of a circular or irregular garden begins with the creation of squares or rectangles. It is a question of the harmonious blending of the two. (GOTD, 25)

·

DOUBLING THE SIZE of the garden by cutting it in half: although this may sound like a paradox, it is plain common sense. A garden is a picture; every picture has a focal point, and if, as it wanders towards the focal point, the eye can be diverted, the picture is thereby apparently enlarged. (GOTD, 26–27)

·

THE MEN WHO write about gardens never tire of telling us to follow Nature and to copy Nature's secrets.... But when I visit their gardens I have a feeling that Nature

cannot have had very much to say to them. Whoever saw a straight border designed by Nature? When did Nature learn the habits of the drill sergeant? (GOTD, 28–29)

.

A GREAT DEAL of weeping goes on in my garden, but it is a happy sort of weeping, for all this bending of branches and bowing of heads is simply due to the fact that so much beauty is displayed on so small a stage. Very few owners of small gardens seem to realize how greatly they can increase the number of trees they are able to accommodate by the simple method of planting those varieties that either weep of their own accord or because we have encouraged them to do so by a little gentle training. (FFF, 76)

.

YOU ARE STANDING in the middle of a square empty lawn, determined to have a heather garden but wondering how on earth you can make it look natural, as though it had arrived there of its own accord.... After endless prowl-ings, mutterings, stickings-in of bamboo stakes, coupled with a great deal of squintings and neck-crickings and even bendings-double to see how it looked upside down through one's legs, I arrived at what seems to me the only solution, which is to make a 'splodge', almost as if you were making a big blot of ink on a sheet of paper. (GOTM, 38–39)

.

THREE CHERRIES, OR five, or whatever the number may be, never two or four. I have always done this myself, instinctively, ever since I planted my first trees. Why? I suppose the answer lies in the fact that one has tried to walk with Nature, and that Nature does not dispose her treasures in squares or in parallel lines. (GOTM, 59)

.

THREE CLUMPS OF red hot pokers are just silly. They look extremely mean and slightly indecent. YOU WANT AN ARMY OF RED HOT POKERS. (AVIAV, 104)

.

THE FEET OF the gardener are of first importance in garden design; indeed, without proper feet, attached to a pair of agile legs, it is difficult to see how a garden can be designed at all. (GOTM, 193–194)

.

HOW IS IT possible to assess the value—in shape, and colour, and general aesthetic significance—of a single branch of a single tree unless one has viewed it from every conceivable angle, in every condition of light and shade, at every time of the year? How can one plot the curve of a single bed unless one has pondered it, and continued to ponder it, time and again—gone to bed with it, dreamt about it? (GOTM, 194)

.

IN CREATING A garden we are creating—or endeavouring to create—a work of art. We are not merely filling in a blank space around the house, nor contriving a playground for tiny tots, nor providing ourselves with enough spinach for our old age. (GOTM, 193)

SELECTING THE PALETTE

PEOPLE HAVE A habit of saying airily that 'flower colours never clash!' I should like them to have heard what a certain scarlet geranium of my acquaintance said to a neighbouring fuchsia, last spring. They might alter their opinion. (DTGP, 130–131)

.

IN SUCH A small space it was essential to get as many reds as possible, or they would have begun to pick quarrels. Two reds always fight; a dozen are always friends. (GGTC, 110)

.

MOST OF THE writers on gardens do not agree that flowers gain in brilliance if they are placed in close proximity to other flowers of the same colour.... This has always seemed to me regrettable, particularly in flower arrangements. White lilies look best against a white wall in a white vase.... The gold of daffodils is enhanced by the gold of forsythia. Green echoes green and complements it. (GOTD, 50)

.

IF YOU GROUP a few bamboos among your autumn-coloured shrubs you will enormously enhance the effect of your reds and your yellows by this background of fresh green. Bamboos are, perhaps, the only evergreens that seem perpetually young. (HDYGG, 32)

.

PARADOXICALLY, BLUE IS a colour that makes many people see red; by which I mean that fierce arguments are constantly developing as to which flower is the bluest.... The caryopteris is radiant in any weather.... The blue of its petals seems to have the quality of carrying for great distances, as though it were some sort of floral evangelist with a message of good tidings for all the world. (FFF, 12)

Caryopteris

IT HAS TAKEN me over thirty years of tireless experiment to discover the glory of grey in the garden, to reach the stage where I can write that it now seems to me as important as any of the colours on the gardener's palette, and maybe even more important. (GOTM, 89)

.

WHITE IS NOT the absence of colour, it is colour in infinite variety, so that an all-white garden is as exciting as the most brilliant border. (GOTD, 139)

.

I WONDER HOW many there are who, when they are picking a rose, realize that the rose leaves are often more brilliant in colour and more delicate in form than the flower itself? (HDYGG, 19)

.

[HOSTA] LEAVES, PROVIDED that you do not throw them away as soon as they begin to turn, have a habit of painting themselves in a long series of subtle, glowing colours. The blue sheen fades away, the edges become rimmed with gold, and the gold spreads over the whole leaf, mottling and dappling it until—come October—you have something that looks as though it has been fashioned in burnished bronze. (FFF, 36)

.

GOLD IN THE garden is worth a lot more than gold in the bank. . . . And just as money breeds money, so, in the garden, gold magnifies gold. (GOTM, 246)

RIPPLES AND REFLECTIONS

JUST AS A room without a mirror is dead, so a garden without water is never quite alive. (MH, 285)

·

THE WATER IN the pool . . . is not only a mirror but a magnet, with a power that reaches to the ends of space. It can pluck the moon from the sky and float it like a lily; it can reach up to the dark night to draw down the stars and hold them shining to its breast; and through all the seasons it paints its pictures of the flowers that lean over it. (MH, 286)

·

ONE OF THE subtlest delights of a water garden is the delight of sound; the sudden 'plop' as a goldfish rises to catch a gnat, the high sharps and trebles of a tiny fountain, the faint buzz of a dragon-fly, the sigh of the wind in the reeds by the edge. (GOTD, 153)

·

ONE IS HEAVY and oppressed, walking across the lawn one's feet drag slowly, one reaches the pool, and stares into the water. And then, even in winter when the lilies are sleeping, something seems to happen. The clouds float at one's feet across the steely surface, the bare branches of the copper beech have the delicate perfection of a Chinese drawing, a bird skims the water, tracing a single exquisite curve, and round the little statue in the centre is spread a liquid tapestry of purest blue. Here is a province of its own, a place of retreat and solitude, where the world's alarms are far away. (GOTD, 26)

IN A MAD moment, I once made a Polythene pond. And the reason why I developed a fierce hatred for it before it was even finished can be summed up in two words— damp underwear. That is what it made me think of, from the very first moment when the Polythene was stretched across the hole. This was not a pool. It was old gentle-men's drawers. (GOTD, 149)

.

I WILL NOT write a long saga about the pool we made. . . . It is the sort of thing which the *Daily Herald* will tell you can be dug over the week-end by a not very bright child with a not very sharp spade. I need hardly say that in fact it required an army of workmen and cost the earth. (MH, 290)

OUTDOOR DECOR

I DON'T LIKE garden ornaments. Somewhere, we may be sure, in one of the suburbs of Purgatory, there is an arid garden where dwell the spirits of all those misshapen creatures who have been decorating so many gardens for so many years. (GGTC, 189)

.

YOU MAY WEAKLY agree, at first, to buy one leaden cupid. The cupid will arrive, looking like a very horrible baby that has been petrified just as it was having an acute attack of wind. You think that perhaps if you get a quickly growing ivy you may be able to cover its revolting nakedness. But you are mistaken. Your purchase of the cupid has caused your name to be entered in the books of the gardening firm as a 'sucker'. (DTGP, 282)

.

THEY WERE DELICATELY carved in lead, and on the sides of each urn four heads were embossed.... Whatever they cost they had to be mine. Repairing the roof could wait; mending the cracks in the ceiling could wait; the peculiar smell in the woodshed could, and almost certainly would, wait. I had to have those urns. (MH, 70)

FOLLOWING THE SCENT

THE SWEET FRAGRANCE of the flowers gives to the mind an amiability in which the most fanciful conceptions flower freely. (DTGP, 235)

.

TAKE THE SCENT of a sunlit nectarine, add a pinch of lemon verbena, sweeten with a drop of the essence of tuberose—and you have a faint idea of the fragrance of the flower of the [grape] vine. (MH, 81–82)

.

JUST BY THE porch there is [a] lemon-verbena, for crunching and sniffing purposes on one's exits and entrances. (It is heart-rending to think that there must be quite large numbers of people who have to go to work every morning without the soothing anodyne of a pinch of lemon-verbena; one cannot imagine how they get through the day.) (CXYZ, 17–18)

.

THERE ARE MELANCHOLY scents—pear blossom that carries with it a feeling that youth is all too transient; there are gay scents, such as the laughing perfume of vine blossoms, which Bacon described as the sweetest of all the garden's essences. There are feminine scents—some of them, like gardenias, so intensely feminine that they are almost embarrassing. And there are masculine scents— moss, bergamot, wood smoke, new-mown hay, and certain

93

vegetables, such as the velvety inside of young broad beans. (GOTD, 158)

.

SCENTED PLANTS, I think, should be disposed strategically. By which I mean that there should be something at the front door, to calm one's goings out and comfort one's comings in, and something at the end of the lawn to sniff, and crunch, and talk about. (GOTD, 159)

.

Azara microphylla is rewarding for an unusual reason, because of its scent. It smells so strongly of vanilla that on sunny days, when little boys walk past the railings of my cottage, they pause and their noses twitch, as though they were saying to themselves: 'The ice-cream man cometh.' (GOTD, 213)

THE EXQUISITELY PRETTY little daphne is fragrant out of doors, on even the coldest morning, under the darkest skies. Some of my happiest memories are of bending down and pushing my nose against its petals, marvelling, as I do so, that this summer fragrance should be stored in the icy heart of winter. (FFF, 20)

·

FOR THE ELDERLY, the whole subject of fragrance in the garden is one to which more attention might be given. The sense of smell is one of the last to desert us and it can give delight and consolation to the end of our lives. Moreover it involves no physical effort. One has yet to hear of anybody dying of exhaustion of the nostrils. (GOTM, 262)

·

THE WORLD NEEDS lavender fans a great deal more urgently than it needs many of the things which it regards as essential. At every international conference there should be lavender fans, to waft sweetness into the dilated nostrils of the participants. There should be lavender fans on the table at every director's meeting, and there should be a large stock of lavender fans at the entrances to the House of Commons and Congress. (SOTL, 240)

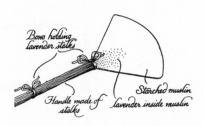

To be 'overpowered' by the fragrance of flowers is a most delectable form of defeat. (MH, 240)

FLORAL HARMONY

The beauty of the moonflower evokes music—the nocturnes of Chopin, the preludes of Debussy, and, above all, the long, haunting cadences of *Swan Lake*. You can hardly ask for more, from a little brown seed. (SOTL, 254)

Chopin, indeed, is our most frequent visitor, from the first snowdrop to the last leaf that drifts from the beeches on a winter's evening. The narcissi dance his mazurkas under the pear tree and throughout the summer his nocturnes echo over the lily pool. For every flower there is a Chopin étude. (GOTM, 151–152)

FLOWERS AND COMPOSERS THIS might make an agreeable diversion for the parlour. Chopin, a narcissus in the rain? Debussy, love-in-a-mist? Rachmaninoff—a creeper of some sort, twisted and tortured, like a wisteria that has been struck by lightning and yet still manages to produce incredible cadenzas of blossom. Beethoven? I suppose that we must settle for the obvious giant oak, even if it is sometimes a blasted oak. (FFF, 8)

.

AS A FRUSTRATED composer I have always regarded gardens in terms of music, and it is perhaps significant that the people who have been the kindest about the few gardens I have been able to design have been musicians. When the late Sir Thomas Beecham stepped on to the lawn at Merry Hall . . . when the balustrades were garlanded in white roses, he exclaimed, 'This is sheer Mozart!' (GOTM, 149)

.

A BLOSSOMING APPLE tree is not merely a blossoming apple tree. It is an étude in D major, in six-eight time, scored mainly in the treble. And across the trunk, when one is contemplating it—particularly if an April breeze is alert among the branches—one mentally scribbles the mood in which the étude is to be played: *Allegro vivace.* (GOTM, 150)

Chapter 8

DOMESTIC AFFAIRS

For Nichols, the garden was an extension of the home and he delighted in showing it to visitors. Hosting social occasions always involved showing guests around the garden and filling the house with cut flowers for them in the colder months. His cats had the run of the home and garden, and were indulged in ways that Nichols did not always extend to his visitors.

BOUQUETS AND DISPLAYS

THERE IS ONLY one 'basic rule' in flower arrangement. And that is to love the flowers, to listen to what they have to say, to watch the way they dance, and then to allow them to express themselves in their own sweet way. (TAOFA, 202)

.

I HAVE ALWAYS tried to let the flowers speak for themselves; I have never asked them to say things which Nature never intended them to say; I have never chopped off their stems, nor twisted their heads, nor tortured their leaves, nor throttled them with wires, nor used any of the loathsome Gestapo tricks of the fashionable florist. (MH, 267)

IF YOU PICK a bunch of Christmas roses, and then pick a few tips of Lawson cypress, and arrange the cypress tips behind the Christmas roses *inside out*, the result is of a beauty indescribable. Because, you see, the inside of the Lawson cypress, which forms the commonest hedge in a million suburban gardens, is delicately flecked with silver. When you put it behind the Christmas roses, the white and silver seem to sing together. It is moonlight calling to moonlight. (SOTL, 245–246)

IF YOU PICK a water-lily in full flower and bring it indoors to float in a bowl, it will look ravishing for a few hours; but then it starts to sulk and close up, and next morning it is giving a very good impersonation of an ill-tempered Jerusalem artichoke. (GOTD, 137)

.

I DO NOT care for artificial flowers. This would be an understatement; I should like to make a bonfire of the whole hard, dusty, chemically-coloured collection. Better a withered dandelion in a jam pot than these bogus monstrosities. (GOTD, 170)

.

EVEN A SINGLE 'shop' carnation in a country bunch seems to put the whole thing out of focus, like a woman in a Dior dress at a meeting of the parish council. (GOTD, 208)

.

EVEN A CLUSTER of dock seeds, if set in the right vase and cunningly lit, can be made to look as exotic as a group of orchids. (TAOFA, 122)

.

VERY FEW SEEM to have grasped the possibilities of the common looking-glass. This seems very odd, if only for economic reasons; after all, six roses in front of a mirror automatically become a dozen roses. (GOTD, 206)

.

I HAD LONG been worried by the difficulty of transporting certain flowers from the country.... The dahlias were the worst.... Then one day ... I had a brain wave. Why not get a small sheet, hang it in the car suspended from the roof, and then pass the stalks of the dahlias through it, so that the blossoms rested on the sheet, without touching one another, and the stalks dangled down into the air? The fact that one would look like the old woman who lived in a shoe if one drove a car so curiously laden did not deter me. (DTGP, 265–266)

THE BUTTERCUP IS 'as tough as they come'. If we pick it kindly and swiftly, and do not linger too long in the sunlight, and if we let it rest in a bucket for the night, it will delight us for a whole week. And if it chooses— when nobody is looking—to let a few petals fall onto the highly-polished mahogany of the Sheraton table where its elegance entitles it to be placed, we should allow those petals to remain, to linger on in a slowly fading gold, to become part of the pattern. (TAOFA, 137)

·

IN ANY FLORAL arrangement, if we study it carefully, we can read some of the secrets of the arranger's heart. (TAOFA, 216)

·

WE CANNOT SOLVE the problems of mankind by arranging flowers; we cannot turn back the tides of war nor set a term to the follies which provoke them. But we can bring a little peace into our own hearts, and shed a little light throughout the domestic circles in which we move and have our being. (TAOFA, 233)

THE PLEASURE OF YOUR COMPANY

I WAS NO longer living in the heart of the country, no longer master of all I surveyed. I was surrounded by quantities of small sovereign states, all intensely nationalist, and populated by mysterious and possibly hostile

tribes who, in the history of Suburbia, are described by
the generic term of 'Neighbours'. (GGTC, 32)

.

WE HAD TWO and a half varieties of ceanothus.... This
enumeration is not perverse: the 'half' was rooted in
the little front garden of my next-door neighbour, Mrs
Poyser, but it had stretched its pretty arms so obligingly
over my own plot that I had come to regard it as partly
mine. (There should be more of this pleasing co-opera-
tion between neighbours.)
(GOTM, 26)

.

A GARDEN CAN MAKE or mar a friendship. It brings out
all sorts of hidden virtues and unsuspected vices.... It is
as though a curious light were reflected from the petals
of the flowers—a light in which the emotions are sharply
revealed. (DTGP, 80–81)

.

WHENEVER YOU ARE showing people over a garden, it is
vital that they should go the longest possible way round.
It may be that there is only one thing in the garden—say
a forsythia—that can lay any claim to excellence ... but
it must not receive attention till the right moment. There
must be a conspiracy of silence about it. If some tiresome guest, stepping out on to the terrace, observes the
forsythia, exclaims with delight, and proceeds to make
a bee-line for it, she must be gently but firmly dragged

Afternoon

back.... The way to the forsythia is arduous and compli-cated.... To look at it too soon is not only impolite. It is positively cruel. (GGTC, 84–85)

·

LONG EXPERIENCE HAS taught me that people who do not like geraniums have something morally unsound about them. Sooner or later you will find them out; you will discover that they drink, or steal books, or speak sharply to cats. Never trust a man or a woman who is not pas-sionately devoted to geraniums. (LOTS, 65)

·

AS A FLOWER [*Iris stylosa*] has only one drawback; it arouses feelings of gross rapacity in one's female friends, who wish to snatch it and pin it to their bosoms and wear it to the opera, where it would certainly die. We must devise our own techniques for dealing with such creatures. (FFF, 43)

THE ANCESTRY [of rosemary] is from the Latin *ros*, which means spray, on account of its liking to grow over the cliffs of the Mediterranean, and *marinus*, which of course means sea. This sort of information, if dropped casually as you are walking round the garden, is calculated to irritate one's dearest friends. (GOTM, 29)

·

ONE OF MY perennial guests is the Bishop of Southwark, who is a party in himself. (The first time he ever called on me he was wearing purple robes, and as soon as he saw the rhododendrons through the window he walked over to them and stood there, looking very magnificent. Then, with great earnestness, he enquired 'Do I match?') (DTKS, 176)

CATTY REMARKS

A FULL LIFE, it will generally be agreed, demands both a garden and a cat, but sometimes (particularly during planting out) life can be almost too full, if your cats are as keen on gardening as mine. Each plant has to be inspected, and if possible rolled upon. And the places where you desire to dig holes are invariably the places which the cat chooses for a long, deep sleep. (GGTC, 241–242)

·

WHEN SEEDS HAVE been sown in the open ground, it is discouraging to look out of the window and see that pussy is using the precise place where they are sown as a public convenience. A nice new seed-bed, to pussy, is an immediate reminder that the time has come for washing the hands or powdering the nose. (CABC, 41)

IF IT IS the month of May, when the blossom is out, and if one is accompanied by a white Persian kitten, which allows itself to be lifted on to a lower branch, in order to dab at twigs, moments of the utmost enchantment are almost certain to ensue. (CABC, 14)

.

THERE IS SOMETHING dead about a lawn which has never been shadowed by the swift silhouette of a dancing kitten. (GOTM, 167)

.

I AM HONOURED by the visits of neighbouring felines. They appear dramatically on the tops of walls, spying out the land (all cats, of course, are in the secret service), or they dart from out of the darkness of the tool-shed. Sometimes they stroll, with apparent nonchalance, across the open lawn, which gives rise to scenes of great tension if any of my own cats happen to be engaged in counter-espionage at the widows, as they often are. (GOTD, 219–220)

.

THERE WERE SEVERAL reasons why it was impracticable to attempt to grow flowers on the top of the wall. There were, in fact, seventeen reasons, some black, some tabby and two ginger. (GGTC, 192)

.

WELL-ESTABLISHED CLUMPS OF heather are in great favour with equally well-established felines, who like to lie in it, dabbing at the bees and pretending to be lions. (GOTM, 44)

.

CATS AND FLOWERS have played so large a part in my life that I can scarcely think of one without the other. In a cluster of wild hyacinths I can see reflected the blue eyes of my first Siamese; on warm May mornings he would wander to the shadow of an old wall where the hyacinths had come by chance, and dispose himself most elegantly upon them. If reproached for squashing the hyacinths, he merely blinked; the blue eyes and the blue flowers, mingling together, were so beautiful that there was nothing to be done about it. (CXYZ, 34)

Midday

Chapter 9

WHO DOES YOUR GARDEN GROW?

That gardeners are often deemed eccentric is not lost on Nichols. But rather than downplay his foibles and follies, he revels in them, freely admitting their existence. Many gardeners have read these confessions with great relief, finding they aren't the only ones with such thoughts and habits.

PECULIAR TO THE SPECIES

SOME FALL IN love with women; some fall in love with art; some fall in love with death. I fall in love with gardens, which is much the same as falling in love with all three at once. For a garden is a mistress, and gardening is a blend of all of the arts, and if it is not the death of me, sooner or later, I shall be much surprised. (MH, 17)

.

EVERY GARDENER HAS a strange and romantic tale to tell, if you can worm it out of him—of blue flowers that came up yellow, or of a white lily that sinned in the night and greeted the dawn with crimson cheeks. In the strong heart of every gardener some wild secret stirs. (DTGP, 132–133)

I THINK THAT gardeners must be like parents. No parent wants to talk about anybody else's child. His own son's adenoids are far more charming to him than any other infant's achievements. And I would rather shake earwigs out of my own dahlias than pick the rarest orchids from the hottest of Sir Philip Sassoon's houses. (DTGP, 189)

.

I ONCE KNEW a man whose wife threatened him with divorce.... He had been away for three months and in his absence she had presented him with a baby. She perversely supposed that his first action, on returning home, would be to come to her room in order to pay his respects to her, and it. Not at all. He found it of more immediate importance to hurry across the lawn to inspect a recently planted *Embothrium coccineum*. This behaviour she found unnatural; some women have no sense of priorities. (GOTM, 18)

.

DO YOU EVER find yourself bursting into a sort of lunatic laughter at the sheer prettiness of things? (GOTM, 114)

.

YOU CAN NO more stop a garden from walking, in spirit, into the house of a gardener than you can stop the sea from flowing, in spirit, into the house of a sailor.... For there is always a little mud on the floor, a feeling of flowers everywhere, a perpetual surge and whisper of branches, and a heavenly scent of flowers. (ATR, 12)

GOOD GARDENERS ARE not quite sane. And all good gardeners will understand me when I refer to this mad urgency to see the garden before it is dark. I think that a large proportion of the road accidents, during the shorter months of the year, must be due to ardent gardeners who are terrified lest they should arrive home too late to 'make the tour'. (AVIAV, 20)

.

I WOULD RATHER have ten square yards of sour soil, surrounded by a hedge so high that it blocked the sun out, than a hundred acres of land without a hedge.... It is not a really very gross exaggeration, and most English gardeners will share it with me.... We cannot explain to foreigners that we have a horror of being seen when we do not wish to be seen. (AVIAV, 67–68)

[MY GARDEN WORKER] was the world's champion waterer. He really loved it.... It is almost as though he were an evangelist, saving souls instead of flowers—as though the sweet brown pond-water, that poured from the can, were a holy water which he had taken from some secret well of the spirit. (AVIAV, 57–58)

·

THE FLOWER SHOW is one of the few places left where it is possible to see a lot of people one knows and yet avoid any danger of having to speak to them, or being asked to lunch, or receiving an invitation to address a public meeting. For the minute one sees an acquaintance in the distance, one can instantly bury one's nose in the centre of a large herbaceous shrub and keep it there, like an ostrich, until the danger is past. (HDYGG, 14)

·

WHENEVER I AM in a garden shop I feel like jumping on the counter and making a speech, because people oughtn't to be allowed to buy such beautiful, precious things as seeds and bulbs if they are only going to maltreat them. (GGTC, 243)

·

I FIND IT DIFFICULT to leave a rose-bed without gathering up the freshly fallen petals; there is something not only wasteful but callous in leaving those fragments of gold and crimson velvet to wither in the sun. (SOTL, 235)

·

I WONDER IF I am the only gardener who has sometimes sunk so low as to nip a seed-pod from a public garden? Obviously it is not a habit to be carried to extremes, but are there not occasions when it might be justified? . . . One says to oneself: 'I came to this place in a heavily taxed car, using heavily taxed petrol, which I paid for out of a heavily taxed income. I am bowed down with taxes, and I need flowers to help me to survive'. . . . So one takes it, and as one does so one goes scarlet in the face and one's heart beats a violent tattoo, and for weeks afterwards every ring at the door suggests a visit from the police. (FFF, 71)

·

LONG EXPERIENCE HAS taught me that whereas people will take advice about love, and about money, and about nearly all the problems which beset us in life, they will scarcely ever take advice about their gardens. (GOTM, 60)

DO YOU SPRING out of bed ... in the middle of the night, in case there is something you may forget? Do you stick up notices like 'Must have a *mass* of grape hyacinths in the drive next year', and tie it round your toothbrush? ... One day I nearly went down into the City having forgotten to remove from my hat a large envelope bearing the strange device, 'Have you sprayed *everything*?' (GGTC, 211)

.

ALL GREAT GARDENERS . . . are also great ramblers; they spend the happiest and most significant days of their lives prowling and poking about and going around in circles. (GOTM, 105)

.

OFTEN, IN THE garden, I have found some plant that has seeded itself in a spot where you would think its frail roots could not possibly gain a hold. Perhaps it is only a common rock-plant that has pitched its gay camp on some wind-swept, barren wall, and is flying its yellow flag in the teeth of every wind. But though it is 'common,' the miraculous courage of such a plant defeats me. I could no more destroy it, even if it is an intruder, than I could tear up a rose tree that was decked in all the crimson regalia of July. (ATR, 24)

.

ONE SEES A woolly caterpillar having an expense-account luncheon off the leaves of a Super Star rose; and one's hard clever hands go out to squash it. And then, suddenly, one does not feel so hard or so clever, and one's fingers falter and a thousand moral problems present themselves. Here is this small furry creature, which has something faintly kittenish about it, and perhaps this may be the crowning moment of its life. (GOTM, 123)

ONE DAY I shall reach an age when I shan't be able to look thirty years ahead in my garden. That will be rather a bitter day. Because all gardeners want to look thirty years ahead. (AVIAV, 175)

LISTENING TO THE FLOWERS

I ALWAYS THINK FLOWERS know what you are saying about them. If I see a scraggly lupin, I like to pass well out of its hearing before delivering any adverse comments on it. For how do we know what tortures it may be suffering? It surely can be no more pleasant for a lupin to have to appear with tarnished petals than for a woman to be forced to walk about with a spotty face. (DTGP, 75)

.

I BELIEVE, WHEN I touch a plant or a tree, that there occurs some contact more subtle and intimate than the mere laying of human hands on vegetable substance, I believe that my blood and the blood of the tree are mingled—green to red, and red to green, as the blood of a man who has died is mingled with the earth. (AVIAV, 274)

.

MY OWN WISTARIA ... has grown right round the window, and in summer, if you want to shut the window, you have to take great care to push away the stem, for the leaves have pushed themselves over the ledge. I feel rather guilty at shutting out so beautiful a thing, when it is obviously anxious to come inside. ... Every summer the wistaria has to be gently told that it has come far enough. (GGTC, 77–78)

.

WHEN MAKING A bunch of mixed flowers from a border, I have sometimes picked one which I don't really want at all, in case it should feel neglected. A habit which no doubt carries sensitivity to the pitch of sickliness. But the world wouldn't be much worse off in these days if a few people *were* a little more sensitive. (GGTC, 268)

HOWEVER SOLITARY YOU may be by nature, however averse to entertaining and giving parties, don't you find that there are times when the sweet peas, as it were, send out their own invitations to tea, or when the irises inform you, in no uncertain voice, that they will be 'at home' next Sunday afternoon? (MH, 192)

·

THERE IS A great deal of truth in the old saying that in a garden the best fertilizer is 'the shadow of the owner'. (MH, 192)

·

THE GREAT MAJORITY of the flowers in my garden are in their present places because they have personally informed me, in the clearest possible tones, that this is where they wish to be. Listening to flowers is one of the most important of all the gardener's duties. (GOTD, 29)

·

I DO INDEED believe that flowers have feelings, and that these feelings extend to the human beings who tend them. If it is true—as it surely is—that there are 'green fingers', to which flowers react in sympathy, why should there not also be 'black fingers', from which flowers—certain flowers—withdraw in distaste? (GOTD, 81)

·

SOME PEOPLE SEEM to forget that a plant is very like a human being. It is much nicer, of course, and much prettier and much pleasanter than a human being, but we are bound to admit the resemblance. (HDYGG, 45)

Chapter 10

SEASONED REFLECTIONS

Underneath Nichols's biting humor and florid descriptions dwells a tendency toward thoughtful contemplation peppered with surprisingly profound observations. His evocations of nature's abounding beauty, its soothing effect and its near-religious spirituality form a philosophy that offers a wealth of garden-related curatives for mankind's ills.

SAFE HAVENS

A GARDENER IS NEVER shut out from his garden, wherever he may be. Its comfort never fails. Though the city may close about him, and the grime and soot descend upon him, he can still wander in his garden, does he but close his eyes. (DTGP, 287)

.

A GARDEN IS LIKE a school—it is a place of youth perpetually renewed—it arouses the same loyalties—it teaches the same lessons....Just as a school is a place of slowly-expanding minds, of quiet adolescent dreams, of the play and inter-play of sweet friendship, so is a garden. (DTGP, 38)

You will find, as you wander through your garden life, that each form of gardening has its separate and peculiar charm—that one corner of your garden will evoke a mood quite distinct from that which pervades you in another. A large garden is like a large house, with rooms variously decorated. There are rooms which soothe and rooms which stimulate, rooms that are only made for work and rooms that are only made for play. (DTGP, 123)

For all the joys that a garden can give you, the chief joy is the excitement which it adds to the wanderer's return.... It must be sad to come home, if you have no garden waiting for you. For then, you have no alternative but to read the silly news-sheets instead of spending your time in the best of all ways, in looking out of the window. (AVIAV, 267–268)

To HAVE POWER, if only for a few hours! That must be the longing of all ghosts who revisit their old homes, who see the havoc that is wreaked by the fools who come after them, who wail disconsolately through ravaged gardens and weep in despair over the woods that their descendants are destroying. For a few hours only, to come back, to issue orders, to set men to work, to enforce obedience, to start the business of salvage, to bring beauty once more into the desert that the others have made. (AVIAV, 283–284)

.

A GARDEN IS A place for shaping a little world of your own according to your heart's desire. (GOTM, 40)

THE WHOLE ESSENCE of a garden is that it becomes an old friend, or rather, a host of old friends. Will the irises be as good this year as they were last? How well will the delphiniums have stood being divided? Will the phloxes have 'established themselves' in the coming summer? These are the things that matter, that really move the heart. (GGTC, 106)

·

A GARDEN IS A mistress whose beauty, far from fading or failing, increases every year. With every passing season she reveals some fresh charm, some new allurement, and one of the greatest delights of gardening—particularly if you keep a diary—is to set down a record of the latest loveliness that time has written on her face. (MH, 239)

·

EVERY LEAF THAT taps against the attic window, every thorn that nestles against the bricks, is part of a barrier that keeps the twentieth century at bay. I have always taken a dim view of the twentieth century, so that I consider this to be a laudable ambition. (MH, 235)

·

ONE OF THE many reasons why gardens are increasingly precious to us in this day and age is that they help us to escape from the tyranny of speed. Our skies are streaked with jets, our roads have turned to race-tracks, and in the cities the crowds rush to and fro as though the devil were at their heels. But as soon as we open the garden gate, Time seems almost to stand still, slowing down to the gentle ticking of the Clock of the Universe. (FFF, 19)

HIGHER POWERS

WHENEVER I GO out into the garden in late November, and look down at the soil from which the tobacco plants have just been uprooted, and see the tens of thousands of tiny seedlings which are already stretching out their small green hands to the dying fires of the wintry sun, I feel puzzled and faintly oppressed by the profligacy of Nature. If it is true that every sparrow falling to the ground is duly registered in a heavenly account book—and I like to hold to this comforting thought—it must equally be true that there is a similar check on every seedling nicotiana. (GOTD, 112–113)

.

THE OBSEQUIES OF flowers, the manner in which they leave the world, slowly divesting themselves of the glories in which they have clothed themselves—these are among the most precious reasons for which we love them. (TAOFA, 137)

.

I HAVE AN *idée fixe*—psychiatrists please note—that it would be pleasing to die to the sound of the wind sighing through the branches of a pine which oneself had planted. (SOTL, 248)

.

I SHOULD NEVER be happy unless some part of me were in the earth—that I must have roots—and that if one foot at least was not in the soil, the other most assuredly would be in the grave. (GGTC, 52)

·

WHATEVER WE MAY find behind the dark curtain, when it falls with our falling lids, when there is silence and the bird-song is stilled, whatever we may find when we step on to the stage where all must play their part—we shall find flowers. (AVIAV, 287)

LIFE LESSONS

IT IS ONLY to the gardener that Time is a friend, giving each year more than he steals. (MH, 187)

·

IT SEEMED TO me that a great many fences had been put up all over the world, in the long course of history, that were not necessary. Fences round nations, fences round property. They were supposed to be symbols of security, but they were cheating symbols. They had a precisely opposite effect from that which was intended. They did not prevent crime, they incited it; they led not to peace but to war. A world without fences would be a better world. (SOTL, 218–219)

.

WHEN YOU ARE concerned with really important things, such as the dew on a spider's web, or the first fragrance of a freesia on a shelf—when you are dealing with such matters, which are infinite and everlasting, it is difficult to look over one's shoulder, as it were, and remind yourself of such shadowy and transient details as the Red Army. In the scale of eternal values, a hundred military divisions are outweighed by a single pinch of thistledown. (MH, 211)

BACKACHE IS AN essential ingredient of success in all the arts, and not only the art of gardening. I doubt if you can even take the backache out of the art of love. (GOTM, 53–54)

SOME PEOPLE FIND importance in the photographs of those titanic mushrooms of atomic poison which are periodically exploded over the world's deserts; I find greater importance in one very small mushroom which mysteriously springs up in the shadow of the tool-shed. (SOTL, 151)

WE BOTH KNOW, you and I, that if all men were gardeners, the world at last would be at peace. (GGTC, 285)

INDEX

The following index lists key words and plant names. In the main text, common names and scientific names have been left as Nichols used them, without corrections or updating. In this index, Nichols's alternate or obsolete spellings of common names appear in parentheses after the currently accepted spelling.

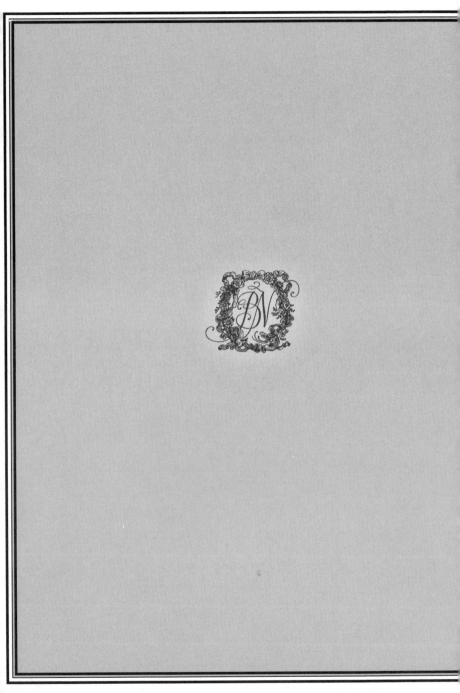